LEI

3

MW01136479

SPECIAL REPORTS

POLICING

IN AMERICA

BY DUCHESS HARRIS, JD, PhD, WITH A.W. BUCKEY

Essential Library

An Imprint of Abdo Publishing | abdobooks.com

abdobooks.com

Published by Abdo Publishing, a division of ABDO, PO Box 398166, Minneapolis, Minnesota 55439. Copyright © 2021 by Abdo Consulting Group, Inc. International copyrights reserved in all countries. No part of this book may be reproduced in any form without written permission from the publisher. Essential Library™ is a trademark and logo of Abdo Publishing.

Printed in the United States of America, North Mankato, Minnesota.
102020
012021

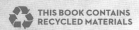
Editor: Alyssa Krekelberg
Series Designer: Maggie Villaume

Library of Congress Control Number: 2020942380

Publisher's Cataloging-in-Publication Data

Names: Harris, Duchess, author. | Buckey, A.W., author.
Title: Policing in America / by Duchess Harris and A.W. Buckey
Description: Minneapolis, Minnesota : Abdo Publishing, 2021 | Series: Special reports | Includes online resources and index
Identifiers: ISBN 9781532194627 (lib. bdg.) | ISBN 9781098214074 (ebook)
Subjects: LCSH: Police--United States--Juvenile literature. | Police-community relations--United States--Juvenile literature. | Police ethics-- Juvenile literature.
Classification: DDC 363.2--dc23

CONTENTS

CHAPTER ONE

SAFE AT SCHOOL?

I t was May 25, 2018, in Noblesville, Indiana. A 13-year-old boy walked into his science class with the intent to kill. He planned to carry out a mass shooting, and he brought two guns to school with him that day. The boy shot his teacher, Jason Seaman, and another student, injuring them both. Seaman was able to grab and subdue the shooter before he hurt anyone else. Another teacher was in the hallway during the shooting and called for a school resource officer—a police officer who worked at the school. The officer immediately went to the scene of the shooting and checked to make sure the student wasn't hiding any more weapons. He also looked after Seaman's injuries before medical help arrived.

Police officers have become more common at schools and university campuses since the 1950s.

The next year, Noblesville was still reeling from the shooting. It was a tragedy that didn't claim any lives, but people there feared the situation could have been much worse. Noblesville decided to nearly triple the number of school resource officers in its schools and put in place other safety measures. Noblesville school resource officers got special training for reacting to emergency situations in schools. Other Indiana school districts followed suit. The Clark-Pleasant school district even voted to establish its first school police force. "It is our local responsibility to keep our kids safe," the district wrote in an announcement.[1]

RESPONDING TO MASS SHOOTINGS

No one is sure exactly how to best respond to the problem of mass shootings. The nonprofit organization Everytown for Gun Safety works to prevent gun violence and advocates for stricter laws on gun ownership and use. The organization recommends taking a few concrete steps to decrease the risk of mass shootings. It advocates for an extreme risk law, which would empower police and others to take guns away from people who show warning signs of committing violence. Other recommended measures, such as banning the sale of powerful guns called assault weapons, would not necessarily involve police.

A DIFFERENT SIDE OF POLICE

Thirty miles (48 km) away and a little over a year after the Noblesville school shooting, there was a very different act of violence at an Indiana school. In August 2019, a fight broke out at Shortridge High, a public high school in Indianapolis. School resource officers called the city police for help, and officers from the Indianapolis Metropolitan Police showed up on campus.

One officer from the department, Robert Lawson, who is white, was filmed confronting a Black woman and teenager outside the school. The video showed the teenager approaching Lawson with his hands down at his sides. Lawson punched the teen in the face. The teenager, a high school student, hit the ground, and Lawson put his knee on the student's torso. Lawson said he struck the teen because he believed the student was about to hit him.

The video went viral on Facebook. It caused outrage and concern in Indianapolis and across the country. Indianapolis Public Schools superintendent Aleesia Johnson said, "It isn't possible to watch the video of the incident that occurred yesterday at Shortridge without immediately thinking about the other incidents in our country that occur between white police officers and Black people."[2] Lawson was eventually arrested for assaulting the student.

EFFECT OF SCHOOL POLICE OFFICERS

Many teenagers are used to seeing police officers in school hallways. According to a 2018 report, during the 2013–14 school year about two-thirds of US high schools had armed police on campus.[3] But school policing is relatively new. The first US police officers in schools started working in Flint, Michigan, in the 1950s. They were called school resource officers, and their role was to serve as mentors and supporters—links between the school and the wider community. These officers were rare in the United States until the 1990s, when strict zero tolerance school

Recent movements for school safety, such as March for Our Lives in March 2018, have focused on gun reform rather than policing.

discipline policies increased the numbers of school police. Additionally, after the 1999 Columbine shooting, when two high school students killed 13 school community members and wounded 20 others, public support grew for school policing.

In 2020, the nonprofit organization Chalkbeat found that school police officers in Indiana were twice as likely to arrest Black students as white ones.[4] Hundreds of these arrests were for minor offenses such as disorderly conduct and tobacco possession—behaviors that many experts argue are better handled as violations of school rules than as crimes. Across the country, the majority of kids arrested at school have committed nonviolent offenses.

ZERO TOLERANCE POLICIES

In schools, zero tolerance policies are rules stating that if people misbehave, they must face certain consequences no matter what. An example of a zero tolerance policy would be a school rule stating that any student caught with alcohol on campus must be suspended for at least two weeks. Zero tolerance policies became popular in the 1980s as a way to combat illegal drug use. Today, many schools have these policies for things such as bringing weapons to school. Schools also use zero tolerance policies for misbehavior such as writing on classroom desks or improperly wearing a uniform. Studies have shown that zero tolerance policies are carried out against students of color much more than white students, leading students of color to face more suspensions or expulsions.[5]

According to a CNN analysis of ten years of mass school shootings, these events are more likely to happen in predominantly white suburbs.[6] The American Civil Liberties Union (ACLU) notes, "Students of color are more likely to go to a school with a police officer, more likely to be referred to law enforcement, and more likely to be arrested at school."[7] Having a disability also increases a student of color's chance of being targeted by police at school. An analysis by the ACLU found that in Rhode Island, male students with disabilities who also have Native American heritage "are arrested at a rate almost 7.5 times the national average."[8]

These differences in treatment help explain why

SCHOOL-TO-PRISON PIPELINE

Students who break rules and face zero tolerance policies can be suspended or expelled. Research done by the US Department of Education Office for Civil Rights shows that Black students are suspended or expelled at disproportionately higher rates than white students, even though there is no evidence that Black students misbehave more.

When students are policed at school, they are more likely to be arrested or develop a criminal record at an early age. That's because when schools involve police in punishments, officers refer students to the juvenile justice system for minor offenses. Then, these students might get a juvenile record. In addition, children and teens who cannot access help for behavioral or substance issues are more likely to be involved with the criminal justice system later in life. Critics refer to the link between harsh punishments in schools and the criminal justice system's involvement as the school-to-prison pipeline.

Students from minority groups are more likely to face discrimination from police officers compared with their white peers.

white students and students of color tend to have different attitudes toward the police. In 2019, a Tulane University study found that 77 percent of white students felt safer with school security present, while only 54 percent of Black students felt that way.[9] High schooler Reagan Razon, who is Black, told CNN, "[Some students] feel like school resource officers are there to protect them from drama or like different dangers. But on the other hand, there's Black students who are really traumatized by the experiences with these officers."[10] Examples of these traumatic exchanges between students and police officers can be found across the United States. For example, in December

2019, a school resource officer in North Carolina and an 11-year-old student, both of whom are Black, were walking down the hallway. The officer grabbed the boy and slammed him to the hallway floor twice. The reasoning behind the officer's actions was not made public. The officer, Warren Durham, was fired and charged with three misdemeanors. The boy was diagnosed with a concussion, and his family expressed dismay that no felony charges were made.

RETHINKING POLICE ROLES

In June 2020, the cities of Minneapolis, Minnesota; Portland, Oregon; and Denver, Colorado, announced that they planned to remove police from schools. These cities' decisions were in response to a national movement. The movement sought to reimagine the role of police not just in schools but in every area of life.

From an early age, many Americans are taught that 911 is the phone number for emergencies. They are told the police are just a call away,

"THE [POLICE] SYSTEM THAT WE HAVE NOW ISN'T WORKING FOR A LOT OF PEOPLE."[11]

— JENNIFER DOLEAC, ECONOMICS PROFESSOR AT TEXAS A&M UNIVERSITY WHO EXAMINES CRIME

Protesters gather in June 2020 and call for campus police at Portland State University to be disarmed.

on hand to help victims of crime and people in danger. In many instances, people are grateful for police aid. However, the fact remains that throughout the country, Black people are disproportionately affected by police brutality.[12] In May 2020, the country appeared to have reached a boiling point. After another Black person's death at the hands of police, outrage swept across the nation. George Floyd died after an officer knelt on his neck for around eight minutes in Minneapolis, Minnesota. This led to a large wave of protests against violence in policing and a countrywide conversation about policing itself.

Police are meant to keep public order, strengthen public safety, and hold criminals accountable while

MORE TO THE
STORY

YOUTH, CRIME, AND POLICING

In the United States, minors are people who are under the age of 18. Minors who are convicted of crimes usually receive different or less harsh penalties than adults do, although there are many cases of minors being tried in court as adults and going to adult prisons. Minors can be arrested just as adults can. In 2018, 728,260 minors were arrested.[13] Of those arrests, most were for nonviolent crimes.

Adolescent brains work differently than adult brains. For example, teenagers are more likely to behave impulsively, or do things without considering the effects of their actions. One research study looked at a case in Massachusetts, where many teens were being arrested for misbehaving on public transportation. To help stop the large number of juvenile arrests, a child psychiatrist and an attorney worked together to create a program that educated police officers on how adolescent brains work. It also tried to show officers better ways to deal with juveniles than by arresting and jailing them. Juvenile arrests decreased dramatically in the years following this program.

protecting victims. The United States has a large, powerful police force, one that is increasingly called on to address a wide variety of social issues. But some Americans do not feel protected by police, and advocates for reform say that policing reinforces social and racial inequalities, often violently. There are various debates on whether some police policies should change. Some argue that qualified immunity, which gives some protections to officers in civil rights cases, should end, while others say it's necessary for police to do their jobs. Another debate centers around police unions and whether they have too much power. And some people question whether community-led police forces would be better than the current forms of policing.

"IT BEARS APPRECIATING . . . THAT AMONG THE RANKS [OF POLICE] ARE HUNDREDS OF THOUSANDS OF HONORABLE MEN AND WOMEN."[14]

—RODD WAGNER, REPORTER

The story of policing in the United States today is a story about justice and injustice, safety and violence. How does the police force protect Americans, and why does it make some people feel unsafe? People question whether there is a way forward that ensures fair treatment and protection for everyone.

CHAPTER TWO

THE HISTORY OF
POLICING

Modern American policing has its roots in European traditions of the 1700s and 1800s, as well as in patrols used to enforce slavery in the American South. Over time, policing in the United States evolved from a shared responsibility to a formal job with its own structure and rules of operation. In the 1900s, urban police officers gained more power, and Black people began to protest unfair treatment and brutality at the hands of the police. The US civil rights movement and social changes of the 1960s and 1970s put new spotlights on policing and inequality, but those decades were also times of widespread support for a strong and well-armed police force.

Some policing in the South focused on keeping people enslaved.

NIGHT WATCHES AND SLAVE PATROLS

When European colonists arrived in North America in the 1600s, they tended to live in small communities, often united by a shared religion or heritage. These early settlements did not have police. Instead, people who broke laws suffered community punishments such as social shunning. As cities started to grow in the colonies, urban leaders saw the need to protect valuable property. At first, some towns and cities used a night-watch system in which residents signed up for part-time, protective night shifts. These night watches eventually evolved into a professional police force. For example, Boston, Massachusetts, created the country's first professional police force in 1838, in part to protect the movement of commercial goods in and out of its large seaport. By the late 1800s, most big cities had police forces.

In the late 1700s and early 1800s, certain areas of the US frontier either didn't have a system to maintain justice or didn't have a functional policing system. Private police groups and nonprofessional crime fighters, called vigilantes, popped up. However, these groups often committed crimes themselves.

In states where slavery was legal, mostly in the South, groups of white men gathered to enforce unjust laws and prevent enslaved people from rising up. The groups these men created were called slave patrols. Both slaveholders and white men who did not enslave people were required to serve on these patrols.

Slave patrols terrorized enslaved people so that they would be afraid to seek freedom. They pursued and captured enslaved people who attempted to escape, often torturing the people they found. In addition, people serving on slave patrols could come to plantations unannounced. They could harm any enslaved person they believed was breaking the law.

W. E. B. DU BOIS AND CIVIL RIGHTS

W. E. B. Du Bois was a writer, speaker, and academic. In the early 1900s, he was the leading Black civil rights activist in the United States. Du Bois helped found the organization called the National Association for the Advancement of Colored People (NAACP), a nonprofit that advocates for civil rights. Du Bois also wrote a book called *The Souls of Black Folk*. The book discussed the mental and emotional toll of living in a society that discriminated against Black people and viewed them through a narrow, stereotypical lens. Du Bois saw the fight against police brutality as another facet of the struggle for civil rights.

CIVIL RIGHTS AND POLICING

In the early 1900s, many Black people began to move from the South, where a large number of police departments were directly descended from slave patrols, into major US cities in the North and West. This period of time is known as the Great Migration (1916–1970). According to Leonard Moore, a professor of history at the University of Texas at Austin, this movement helped shaped policing in the United States:

> Most white communities, including white police departments, were unaccustomed to the presence of African Americans and reacted to their increasing numbers with fear and hostility, attitudes that were exacerbated by deeply ingrained racist stereotypes. Reflecting the beliefs of many whites, northern police departments acted upon the presumption that African Americans, and especially African American men, possessed an inherent tendency toward criminal behavior, one that required constant surveillance of African Americans and restrictions on their movements (segregation) in the interests of white safety.[1]

At the same time, lynching posed a serious threat to the safety of Black people. Lynching is when a person is murdered by a mob. Almost 5,000 of these violent incidences were recorded between 1882 and 1968.[2]

Most of the people lynched were Black. These murders were rarely investigated by police, and the people who committed them were usually not brought to justice.[3]

As policing became widespread, major US cities developed a tradition of staffing police departments with officers who were loyal to the city government and came from the neighborhoods they served. This meant that police officers were often involved community members, even setting up services such as soup kitchens and homeless shelters for local residents. It also meant that officers often felt no obligation to protect those they saw as outside their own communities, leaving minorities and newcomers especially vulnerable. By the 1920s, early civil rights leaders were

AUGUST VOLLMER, FORENSICS, AND POLICE REFORM

August Vollmer was a police chief and professor of criminology. He started his policing career in Berkeley, California, in the early 1900s and later became the police chief of Los Angeles. When he started his career, Vollmer saw police officers as corrupt and violent. He wanted to create a police force that formed deep bonds with community members in order to help fight crime. Vollmer advocated for a college-educated police force and helped create the first college program for police officers.

Vollmer was interested in applying scientific techniques to policing, establishing the first police crime lab in 1923. The lab used technologies such as fingerprinting and handwriting analysis to help find criminals. Vollmer hired Black police officers and female police officers in a time when it was uncommon to employ people from either demographic.

protesting acts of police violence against Black people. In 1929, an investigation into the Chicago-area police found that while Black people made up 5 percent of Chicago's residents at the time, they made up 30 percent of the people who were killed by police.[4]

The civil rights movement of the 1950s and 1960s helped put spotlights on police brutality and racism. During civil rights protests in Alabama, photographs of police officers using dogs and fire hoses against peaceful

During the 1965 Watts Riots, demonstrators pushed over police cars to show their frustration.

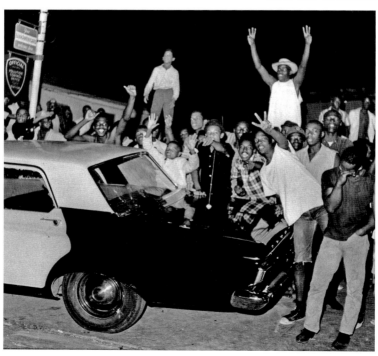

protesters shocked the country. Riots also ignited around the nation.

In 1965, massive riots began in Los Angeles, California. A Black driver was arrested by a white officer in the Watts neighborhood. Long-standing tensions between the police and people in the majority-Black neighborhood led to violence in the crowd that spiraled into more widespread riots, often referred to as the Watts Riots.

The California state government called in thousands of National Guard troops and enforced a curfew, or a mandatory time to stay indoors, in the area. Some people saw the demonstrations as symbols of protest for social change and proof that the government needed to do more to address widespread racial and economic inequality. For others, they were worrisome reminders of the dangers of lawlessness and inadequate policing. In response to the riots, police departments across the country began to expand their budgets and equipment to deal with protests and civil unrest.

MORE TO THE
STORY

SWAT TEAMS

Special Weapons and Tactics (SWAT) teams are small groups of police officers armed with special militaristic equipment. The teams were created in Los Angeles in the 1960s in response to the Watts Riots. Los Angeles Police Department leadership believed that these teams could help control any future riots and help protect police in high-risk situations, such as hostage negotiations.

SWAT teams have distinctive appearances, with officers often wearing heavy protective gear and moving around in armored vehicles. SWAT teams can be found across the country and became better funded even as crime decreased. By 2017, there were 50,000 SWAT raids a year in the United States.[5] Many SWAT teams experienced heavy criticism for using excessive force and for their high operating expenses. In 2014, the SWAT team of Hallandale Beach, Florida, a town with a population of about 40,000, killed an unarmed Black man in a drug raid, and none of the officers involved faced charges.[6] Public outrage followed. In 2020, the team disbanded after ten of its members resigned. The team said it felt unsupported and underfunded by its local government.

TOUGH ON CRIME

The late 1960s through the 1980s was a time of high crime in the United States. Serial killings were at an all-time high during this period, and rates of crimes such as murder and robbery spiked in major cities. Many people wanted a solution to the crime problem and protection from violence.

In 1971, President Richard Nixon announced his plan to combat crime by launching the War on Drugs campaign. Law enforcement shifted its focus to comply with this and began using aggressive tactics to find and target drug users and sellers. The president's administration knew that most drug users were not violent. However, Nixon thought that a tough drug policy would be popular with voters, many of

MIRANDA WARNING

The Fifth Amendment of the US Constitution states that people have the right to not self-incriminate, or say something that would help prove they committed a crime. In 1966, a Supreme Court case called *Miranda v. Arizona* ruled that police officers who wanted to question a suspect they had arrested were required to remind the suspect of her or his Fifth Amendment rights. Today, officers must give what is called a Miranda warning to people they arrest: "You have the right to remain silent. Anything you say can and will be used against you in a court of law. You have the right to an attorney. If you cannot afford an attorney, one will be provided for you. Do you understand the rights I have just read to you? With these rights in mind, do you wish to speak to me?"[7]

President Richard Nixon implemented a War on Drugs policy that included strict criminalization of marijuana.

whom associated drug use with other criminal behavior.

After Nixon, other presidents embraced this same logic and used an antidrug approach to signal that they took public safety seriously.

The War on Drugs continued for the next few decades, empowering police to use combative tactics to

"I HAVE FOUND GREAT AUDIENCE RESPONSE TO THIS [LAW AND ORDER] THEME IN ALL PARTS OF THE COUNTRY, INCLUDING AREAS . . . WHERE THERE IS VIRTUALLY NO RACE PROBLEM AND RELATIVELY LITTLE CRIME."[8]

—RICHARD NIXON IN A PRIVATE LETTER, 1968

pursue drug offenders. The Cato Institute is a research organization that focuses on public policy. In 2017, it released an analysis saying that the War on Drugs had failed and that the combative tactics used on drug offenders had a trickle-down effect. "As a result of violent drug interactions, police are more likely to adopt more intense techniques and stronger equipment. As these practices become ingrained in everyday policing, citizens outside the illicit drug market will also be affected," the report said.[9]

THE FBI

While police handle law enforcement at the state or local level, there are also law enforcement agencies at the federal level. The Federal Bureau of Investigation (FBI) is one of the most well-known federal law enforcement agencies. President Theodore Roosevelt, who once served as the head of the New York City police, founded the agency that later became the FBI. The FBI was founded in 1908. Its purpose is to investigate federal crimes, such as terrorism. The FBI is also responsible for enforcing laws against theft and corruption inside and among businesses. FBI employees are called agents rather than officers.

CHAPTER THREE

WHAT DO THE
POLICE DO?

Police officers are members of law enforcement who work for the government at the state and local levels. Police officers have two main jobs: to maintain a general sense of order and to investigate and prevent crimes. This work is complex. The police must choose which laws to enforce, as well as how and when to enforce them.

Laws serve many purposes. Some laws exist in order to reflect common, shared ideas about right and wrong, whereas others are designed to keep society running according to certain rules. In the US legal system, crimes that are considered serious, such as attacking and injuring someone, are classed as felonies. Less serious crimes, such as verbal harassment, are misdemeanors.

The role of police officers is to make sure that laws are enforced and communities are protected from crime.

K-9s

Some police departments have trained dogs to help with police work. Dogs have an excellent sense of smell, and trained dogs can detect the presence of illegal drugs or explosives, such as hidden bombs. Police dogs are called K-9s, a play on the word *canine*. K-9 police officers get special training to work with dogs. In addition, K-9 police dogs work as public relations tools. Police departments can use the dogs to generate positive attention for police work, whether by allowing the community to interact with police dogs or by posting information and updates about the dogs through media.

"FELONY ARRESTS OF ANY KIND ARE A RARITY FOR UNIFORMED OFFICERS, WITH MOST MAKING NO MORE THAN ONE A YEAR."[3]

—ALEX VITALE, SOCIOLOGY PROFESSOR AT BROOKLYN COLLEGE

Actions that break rules of public order, such as parking violations, are called infractions. Police are responsible for enforcing state and local laws at all levels. However, they get a certain amount of leeway in deciding which laws to prioritize and how they should treat people who break the rules.

POLICE IN AMERICA

In 2018, 661,330 people worked as police officers.[1] Racial minorities and women were underrepresented in police leadership, with only 10 percent of police supervisors being women and 20 percent being Black or Hispanic.[2]

Most US police departments are quite small, serving residents of towns with fewer than 10,000 people. Only

3 percent of police departments serve major cities where more than 100,000 people live.[4] While a typical police station in the United States might have just a small handful of officers, large city departments tend to have significantly higher budgets, more personnel, and more equipment.

Policing is a relatively well-paid job. In 2020, police officers in the United States made an average salary of $67,600 a year. This is significantly higher than the national average salary of $51,960.[5] In addition, many police officers earn above their baseline salaries by working overtime, or more than 40 hours a week, at an increased hourly rate. Most police officers are eligible for early retirement after 20 years on the job. Retired officers typically receive pensions, or portions of their salaries each year, as money to live on after retiring.

UNPOLICED TOWNS

Some small towns do not have the resources to hire police. In rural North Dakota, for example, many towns share the services of a sheriff's department instead of having their own police forces. Some very remote areas have trouble recruiting officers to move there and work full-time. In Alaska, more than 70 villages have no police officers, and many villages resort to hiring officers with a history of committing crimes. Rates of sexual assault are high in western Alaska, and many villages lack the resources to help victims quickly and effectively. Police officers in the area talk of feeling overwhelmed and overworked.

The combination of a decent salary and good benefits makes policing an attractive job option for many people.

HOW TO BECOME A POLICE OFFICER

Police officer applicants typically must have a high school degree or an equivalent degree and be in good physical health. They also have to be US citizens, be over the age of 21, and have good vision. Police officers are screened to make sure they don't have criminal records or histories of poor performance at work.

Firearm training is just one part of the process of becoming a police officer.

The process to become a police officer typically starts with an exam that tests the applicant's reading, math, and memorization abilities. After passing the exam, would-be officers go through a multistep interview process to test their physical and mental health and ability to do the job. Once they are hired by a department, officers start probation periods where they are trained on the details of the job.

DAILY LIFE OF POLICE OFFICERS

Police officers have many responsibilities. They are expected to respond to crimes and emergencies. They are also tasked with trying to prevent crimes. Police officers in small communities tend

PRIVATE INVESTIGATORS

People or organizations can hire private investigators to do research and surveillance on individuals or companies. Private investigators are not formal law enforcement officers. Instead, they work directly for clients and can investigate noncriminal situations or work on legal matters. For example, a law firm might hire a private investigator to help it gather evidence on a case. Private investigators usually need high school diplomas in order to practice, and they have to be licensed in the state where they practice. Many retired police officers choose private investigation as a second career.

"AT THE END OF THE DAY, OUR GOAL IS TO HELP PEOPLE. . . . MY GOAL ISN'T JUST TO BECOME A POLICE OFFICER JUST TO ARREST PEOPLE AND LOCK UP THE BAD GUYS."[6]

—DARRY JONES, POLICE OFFICER IN COLUMBIA HEIGHTS, MINNESOTA

to cover a wide range of official duties, whereas larger police departments may have officers who specialize in specific tasks. For example, crime scene investigators specialize in analyzing the evidence at a crime scene, and they typically have special skills and training.

Most police officers, however, do not have specialized jobs. In fact, most officers do not focus on addressing criminal matters in their day-to-day work. The bulk of policing arrests are for low-level offenses or for infractions such as disorderly conduct, which can include behaviors such as being noticeably drunk in public or hanging around a private business with nothing to do. Police can try to connect and check in with local residents and business owners, keep

MORE TO THE
STORY

INTERNAL AFFAIRS
INVESTIGATIONS

Large police departments have internal affairs divisions responsible for investigating police misconduct. Misconduct could include breaking department rules, mistreating citizens, or engaging in corruption, such as accepting bribes from organized crime organizations. Citizens can make complaints against police officers' behaviors, and officers can also file complaints against other officers. These complaints are supposed to be investigated by officers within the department. In about half of US states, it is difficult or impossible for the public to access the results of those investigations.

Critics of the internal affairs system argue that it's a conflict of interest to have police officers investigate other officers. Former police officer Larry Smith thinks that police departments aren't able to be objective about police misconduct. "Police investigating other police is just a bad idea," Smith argues.[8] However, others note that these investigations are often conducted by officers who have experience with investigative work and are therefore suited for the task.

an eye out for people who may be behaving in strange or inappropriate ways, or stay available so they can quickly respond to emergencies.

Police officers have a lot of choices in responding to tense situations or potential disturbances. If they see crimes being committed, police officers can choose to make arrests. They can also talk to people they think are behaving dangerously, or they can let people who commit small offenses go with just a warning. Police can ask

The majority of police interactions do not require force, but officers may still be armed.

questions of people they suspect of committing, assisting with, or knowing about crimes. However, in most cases, citizens have the right not to answer these questions if they choose not to. Police have the right to pat down people they suspect of having weapons, but usually they cannot search people or go through their things without warrants. Police must follow guidelines on the use of force, making sure that they do not harm people any more than they believe they have to in order to maintain safety and order. Police officers who violate these rules may face professional or legal consequences.

Officers carry firearms with them, even in situations where they don't anticipate any danger or where violence is unlikely. Policing is a dangerous job. According to the Bureau of Labor Statistics (BLS), in 2018, 108 officers died on the job. This was almost a 14 percent increase from the year before and is much higher than in other occupations.[9] The BLS states most officers die from traffic incidences and violence, such as gun violence.

FROM THE
HEADLINES

POLICE OFFICERS OF COLOR

Police officers come from all backgrounds and walks of life. For police officers of color, the positives of the job often come alongside an awareness of policing's history that includes racism. For instance, Virginia officer David Hughes, who is Black, has faced racist attitudes from other officers throughout his career, but he believes that policing is a valuable community service. Hughes supports several police reforms and believes that US cities should make a strong effort to hire a police force that is as diverse as the population it serves.

New York City police recruits stand to take their oaths of office.

Some Black police officers don't see a conflict between the demands of the job and policing's reputation as being antiblack. "I've never been torn. I'm able to be a Black woman and a police officer and do my job professionally as I was trained," says Cheryl Dorsey, a retired Los Angeles police officer.[10] During her career, Dorsey testified against a fellow officer who killed a Black civilian.

CHAPTER FOUR

POLICE FUNDING, POWER, AND INFLUENCE

P olice departments vary greatly in size and influence. There are no official guidelines for how many police officers or how much equipment a city should have, and two cities of the same size may have very different police departments. In general, however, the police departments of medium and large US cities have significant financial resources and a great deal of political and cultural power. In most big cities, police departments receive a larger chunk of the city budget than other services. Police departments can profit from the work they do, gaining a percentage of fees from traffic fines and other offenses that come

Larger cities, such as New York City, receive more funding for their police departments than smaller cities and those in rural areas.

with a monetary penalty. In addition, police can get more money through a process called civil forfeiture. Police unions can wield a great deal of power in the areas where they're most active. And books, movies, and other popular media help shape the image of policing in many people's minds, which can alter people's perceptions of police.

POLICE FUNDING AND CIVIL FORFEITURE

Police officers are public servants, which means that the money supporting their work and paying their salaries ultimately comes from the government, not from private companies. City budgets, which are funded by taxpayer money, are responsible for providing police with their salaries, operating expenses, and equipment. In 35 of the 50 biggest US cities, policing is the largest item on the city's operating budget, and most of the money for police goes toward paying officers' compensation. For example, in 2020, four major Texas cities—Houston, Dallas,

"WE'RE ASKING THAT THE MONEY THAT THE CITY COUNCIL CONTINUES TO GIVE TO THE POLICE DEPARTMENT, LET'S FUNNEL [SOME OF THAT MONEY] BACK TO THE SCHOOL DISTRICT."[1]

—MEAGAN HARRIS, A TEACHER IN ROCHESTER, NEW YORK, ON BUDGET PRIORITIES IN HER CITY

San Antonio, and Austin—each spent more than a third of its general fund, or overall money, on police.[2]

There are other avenues for police departments to fundraise. One such method is civil forfeiture. Civil forfeiture laws allow law enforcement bodies, such as police and prosecutors' offices, to take property that they believe was involved in a crime. For example, police could seize a home where they suspect illegal drug sales took place, even if they do not have definite evidence and even if the owners of the house were not involved. The people who own the property do not have to be convicted, or even suspected, of a crime in order for their belongings to be seized.

For example, in 2016, a man in Texas lost possession of his car because police believed that its hidden compartments might contain drugs. There were no drugs, but the department kept the car. Once the property belongs to the state, police departments are usually entitled to a large share of its value. There are very few limits on how police departments can spend civil forfeiture money. Citizens who believe their property has been seized unfairly can fight the police's decision, but it is a tough and expensive process.

POLICE UNIONS AND QUALIFIED IMMUNITY

A labor union is a group of workers in a particular industry who band together to fight for their interests, such as better pay and working conditions. In major cities, police unions advocate for the financial and professional interests of police officers, and these unions can be quite powerful. Unions are valuable resources for some officers. They often provide officers with counseling services, disability benefits, life insurance, and legal counsel.

In June 2020, protesters in Chicago call for changes to be made in police departments.

Unions are designed to benefit officers and not the community as a whole. It's in the best interests of police unions to fight budget cuts to police departments, especially since the bulk of the money in the budget goes toward officer pay. Unions also advocate for protections that make it more difficult to fire their workers. This means police unions have an incentive to fight against accountability measures such as making police records public or adding harsher consequences for police misconduct. In many major US cities, police unions have sway over local politicians. They can also use organizing tactics such as strikes to influence government decisions.

During a strike, workers in an industry refuse to go to work until their demands are met. Workers can also deliberately slow down, becoming less efficient and more difficult to cooperate with.

REPEALING 50-A

In 1976, New York passed a law called 50-a that allowed police officers and other public employees to keep their personnel records private. Police officers get performance reviews, and records are made of any complaints made against them. These records can help the public understand how well police officers do their jobs. They can also help citizens understand how incompetent or abusive officers are held accountable. In 2020, after the killing of George Floyd and police brutality protests across the United States, many New Yorkers called for the law to be repealed, or taken away. In June 2020, it was.

Police unions have been accused of using this tactic in response to proposed changes or budget cuts. For example, Minneapolis city councilmember Steve Fletcher believes that he faced retaliation from police unions for voting to give the police less money. After his vote, people in his community told him that the police response to calls in the area had slowed drastically. "[Minneapolis Police Department] officers [told] business owners to call their councilman about why it took so long," Fletcher said.[3]

> "THE ELEPHANT IN THE ROOM WITH REGARD TO POLICE REFORM IS THE POLICE UNION."[4]
>
> **—JACOB FREY, MAYOR OF MINNEAPOLIS**

Another policy called qualified immunity allows police officers some protection when they violate the rights of citizens. When police violate peoples' rights to freedom and privacy, such as by not respecting suspects' right to remain silent or searching possessions without probable cause, they can be accused of wrongdoing and sued in court. Qualified immunity states that police and other government officers are not responsible for violating citizens' rights unless they had reasonable knowledge that what they were doing was a violation of the law.

In practice, this policy is interpreted broadly. Police are often immune from accusations about violating people's civil rights if there hasn't already been a court case that's almost exactly the same. For example, in 2014, officers ordered police dogs to attack and bite a suspect who had already surrendered. The man sued, and it turned out that there was a previous case where police had violated a surrendered suspect's rights by ordering a dog to bite him. But since the first case involved a man who was lying down, and the second man had been sitting up, the court ruled that the two cases were not similar enough. It ruled police officers could not have reasonably known what they did was unconstitutional.

POLICE SUPPORT IN POPULAR CULTURE

Movies, TV shows, and books about police work and criminal investigations are extremely popular in US culture. Many of these show police in a very positive, exciting light. In fact, Hollywood productions often work closely with police officers, getting their approval and help with certain aspects of production, such as fact-checking scripts and borrowing equipment. Critics sometimes refer to these productions as *copaganda*—a play on the term *propaganda*, or material designed to aggressively promote a certain idea or point of view.

Many entertainment media portrayals of police are not accurate reflections of police work. They often give the impression that detective work and felony investigations, alongside high-action pursuits and confrontations with violent criminals, make up the bulk of policing. They also have vastly different portrayals of police behavior. For instance, some TV shows depict police brutality and corruption. Others, such as the comedy TV show *Brooklyn Nine-Nine*, show very different cop characters who are silly or incompetent.

Brooklyn Nine-Nine is one of many popular TV shows about cops.

Even nonfiction portrayals of policing tend to sensationalize the daily lives of police. The TV show *Cops* was one of the most popular windows into the world of US policing during the 33 years it ran on TV. *Cops* was a reality show that launched in 1989, and it aired actual footage of police chases, arrests, and other interactions with civilians. *Cops* was widely criticized for stoking fears about violent crime, showing ordinary people in negative lights, and perpetuating racism. TV critic John O'Connor said the show's very first episode was already painting a damaging portrayal of race: "The overwhelmingly white troops of police are the good guys; the bad guys are overwhelmingly Black."[5]

THE MEDIA AND STEREOTYPES

The media can affect people's perceptions about reality, and this is evident when it comes to race. If people aren't around certain racial groups, they tend to internalize messages seen in the media about that racial group. For example, if a white person who has only ever lived in a white community watches a TV show that depicts Hispanic characters as illegal immigrants who commit crimes, the viewer may start to believe those stereotypes. He or she may begin to assume that all people of that race are criminals.

Media stereotypes can also harm an individual's sense of self-worth. The Scholars Strategy Network is a nonprofit organization run by researchers and academics. It notes, "Researchers have found that prolonged television exposure predicts a decrease in self-esteem for all girls and for Black boys, but an increase in self-esteem for white boys. These differences correlate with the racial and gender practices in Hollywood, which predominantly casts white men as heroes, while erasing or subordinating other groups as villains, sidekicks, and sexual objects."[6]

CHAPTER FIVE

RACE, CLASS, AND POLICING

Americans are not policed equally. Racial discrimination has been present throughout the entire history of US policing. Many inequalities in arrests, police encounters, and incidents of police violence are directly linked to War on Drugs policies that targeted racial minorities, particularly Black, Hispanic, and Native American people, at disproportionate rates.

In addition, people with low incomes are at an increased risk of experiencing police violence and harassment. In the United States, there is a significant wealth gap between people of different races. A long history of racial oppression in employment, education, housing, health care, and general opportunity means

A woman at a protest in Washington, DC, holds up a sign filled with names of Black people who have died over the years due to police violence.

that Black and Hispanic people tend to make less money and have less saved and inherited wealth than white people do. People in race-class subjugated communities—areas where a majority of people both have low incomes and are Black, Hispanic, or Native American—are at especially high risk of police violence and arrest.

There is another dimension to the story of race and class inequality in US policing. In the early 1900s, Black people found themselves both overpoliced and underpoliced. This meant they were disproportionately targeted for police violence and arrest and also unprotected by law enforcement when victimized by violent crimes such as lynching. Today, this same dynamic exists, especially in race-class subjugated communities. While

INNER CITIES AND WHITE FLIGHT

The United States was once segregated by race until it became unlawful to actively do so. Today, even in diverse areas, many neighborhoods and towns are unofficially separated along racial lines. In the first part of the 1900s, many Black people moved from the American South to the North in a shift known as the Great Migration. In these large northern cities, they were able to access more job opportunities, but they also faced significant discrimination, including unfair housing policies. Partly as a result of Black people moving to these areas, many middle- and high-income white Americans left big cities for the suburbs, a phenomenon called white flight. Today, many cities still have large, predominantly Black neighborhoods, often in areas considered less desirable, along with majority-white, higher-income suburbs.

people in these communities tend to have many more interactions with police than people in higher-income or majority-white communities, they also tend to lack support from law enforcement.

THE WAR ON DRUGS AND UNEQUAL POLICING

The War on Drugs helped create aggressive policies designed to catch and punish all cases of drug possession and sale, no matter how minor. These policies were often enacted in discriminatory ways. For example, research shows that white and Black people use drugs at similar rates but that Black people are almost three times more likely to be arrested on drug charges than white people.[1]

Another example of racist outcomes in policing comes from the stop-and-frisk policies in New York City. Stop-and-frisk refers to a police officer stopping a civilian on the street, frisking the person—or patting her or him down to check for things such as drugs or weapons—and then asking the person questions. Rudy Giuliani, who was New York City's mayor from 1994 to 2001, adopted the stop-and-frisk policy. This policy was designed to help reduce crime, and it said that New York Police Department (NYPD) officers could stop and frisk people on the street if they had reasonable suspicion the people might be involved in something illegal.

This guideline was so vague that officers were able to stop virtually anyone at any time. The New York Civil Liberties Union recorded more than five million stop-and-frisks of New Yorkers between 2002 and 2019. Each year, more than half of those stopped were Black and about 30 percent were Hispanic.[2] The

Protesters fill the streets in 2012 in New York City, calling for an end to the stop-and-frisk program. Police often targeted people of color.

population of New York City is about 24 percent Black and 30 percent Hispanic.[3]

In 2013, a New Yorker named Keeshan, who is Black, said he had been stopped and frisked by police more than 100 times between the ages of 13 and 18. That same year, a judge ruled that New York's stop-and-frisk program was unconstitutional. However, the New York Civil Liberties Union

noted that the stops continued, although at a decreased rate. Around 90 percent of those stopped and frisked were innocent of any illegal activity.[4]

POLICE VIOLENCE AND RACE

According to data by Mapping Police Violence, over the years of 2013 and 2019, more than 1,000 people who were unarmed died as a result of police violence. Approximately one-third of these individuals were Black.[5]

According to a 2019 publication in the scientific journal *Proceedings of the National Academy of Sciences* (*PNAS*), Black men and women, Native American and Alaska Native

SEX-RELATED CRIMES AND POLICE

Women are significantly less likely than men to be killed by police. According to a 2019 article in the PNAS, "The average lifetime odds of being killed by police are about 1 in 2,000 for men and about 1 in 33,000 for women"—a stark difference.[8] However, some women, as well as boys who are often children or teenagers, suffer sexual assault at the hands of police. According to 2018 research by Bowling Green State University, police officers were charged with rape 405 times and of forcible touching 636 times between 2005 and 2013.[9] However, many criminal justice experts think that number is lower than the actual figure because people may not report the assault.

men and women, and Latino men have a greater likelihood of being killed by police than white people do. The study also found that Asian and Pacific Islander women and men and Latina women are at the lowest risk for police killings. In addition, Black people are significantly more likely to suffer from nonlethal forms of police violence, such as beatings or handcuffing without arrest.

POLICE BIAS

Joseph Cesario is a psychologist at Michigan State University. He looked at deadly police shootings that took place in 2015, and in 2019 he reported that "the race of a police officer did not predict the race of the citizen shot. In other words, Black officers were just as likely to shoot Black citizens as white officers were."[7] The findings were published in PNAS.

In the same study, David Johnson, who is from the University of Maryland, says the findings were significant because people have a tendency to incorrectly assume it's only white officers who shoot and kill people of color. However, Johnson notes that it's important for people to continue paying attention to race, bias, and the effects those have on policing. Lorie Fridell is a bias trainer and a criminologist, and she notes that, "People can have biases against their own demographic groups. Women can have biases about women. Blacks can have biases about Blacks. It is incorrect to assume that any issue of bias in policing is brought to us by white males."[10]

Police training plays a role in how officers respond to certain situations. Larry Smith is a former police officer who worked in Baltimore, Maryland. Smith remembered that in his police training, he was taught to always protect his gun from the people he met. He said his training also taught him to see all citizens as threats. Even the first aid training he got later in his career focused on helping other police officers, not the people he served. "The narrative in all this was saving ourselves and other cops—but not citizens," Smith said.[11]

Everyone has biases of some kind. Bias may be conscious or unconscious—known and understood or hidden and unrecognized. Racial bias occurs when people think about others differently and treat them differently due to their race. Some police officers are aware of their biases and broadcast them openly.

In 2017, a group of Philadelphia, Pennsylvania, lawyers decided to look into the public social media posts of law enforcement officers. They launched a database called the Plain View Project. The project collected a database of thousands of posts and comments that expressed bigoted views or called for violence against people who hadn't been charged with crimes. Some posts used racial slurs or racist insults, such as comparing Black people to animals. It's not illegal for police officers to express racist views in their private lives, but openly racist officers are unlikely to treat all citizens equally and gain the trust and respect of citizens.

A person may feel that racism is wrong but still absorb racist ideas, often without being aware of having done so. Racial stereotypes are widespread in US society. There is a long history of stereotyping Black men in particular as more likely to commit crimes and violence. Law professor Katheryn Russell-Brown calls this the criminal Black man stereotype. It is widely reinforced through media such as video games, movies, TV shows, and news reports. Research suggests that many Americans, including police officers, have absorbed this harmful stereotype.

In the early 2000s, a psychologist named Joshua Correll designed a test of implicit bias and violence. He made a video game that showed players images of white and Black people in different physical postures, some holding everyday items and others holding guns. Correll asked test subjects to press a button to pretend to shoot the people who were holding guns. Correll found strong evidence of bias. People who played the game—Black as well as nonblack, and both police

THE SUPERPREDATOR MYTH

In the 1990s, criminologist John DiIulio coined a name for a new racial stereotype of young Black men and youth: the superpredator. According to DiIulio, superpredators were teenagers and young men who completely lacked empathy, were incapable of thinking about the future, and would kill without any regret. He described these young people as most likely to be found in low-income, majority-Black areas. However, it turned out there was more to the story. Researchers at the University of Cincinnati found that many of these people had been exposed to lead as children, damaging their brains. The banning of lead paint and gasoline helped bring down juvenile crime.

officers and members of other professions—were more likely to shoot at images of unarmed Black people than images of unarmed white people. Other psychologists have found that these implicit biases have an effect on how people behave in real-life situations. Today, many police departments host implicit bias training programs to help officers unlearn deeply rooted prejudices.

Ann Bozzi instructs a group of Los Angeles police officers on implicit bias and how prejudices can affect their work.

STRUCTURAL RACISM AND POLICING

The terms *structural racism* and *systemic racism* refer to racism that pervades a society, so that not only individual interactions but also larger systems such as health care, law, education, and policing produce unfair outcomes and treat people unequally based on race. Individual people do not have to have racist intentions or beliefs in order to reinforce a racist system.

One reason for structural racism is the way the policing system is set up. It rewards officers for making a lot of arrests. At the same time, officers can face pressure to ignore or downplay serious crimes, especially in high-crime areas, to make their policing work seem more effective. The podcast *Reply All* reported on a case of attempted police reform that ended up reinforcing social inequalities. In the 1990s in New York City, when crime rates were very high, officers often ignored reports of crime in race-class subjugated neighborhoods, preferring to focus on the

"ACROSS RACE, MOST PEOPLE FEAR YOUNG, AFRICAN-AMERICAN MALES."[12]

—KATHERYN RUSSELL-BROWN, CRIMINOLOGIST AND LAW PROFESSOR

problems of wealthier citizens. One officer, Jack Maple, wanted to find a way to target small groups of criminals, such as small bands of subway muggers, who were causing disproportionate amounts of crime. He used his talent for observation and pattern recognition to find ways of pinpointing crime hot spots and arresting the people responsible.

Maple wanted to get New York City's police department on board with his way of fighting crime. He became deputy commissioner of crime-fighting strategies and created a system called CompStat, which measured how vigorously police officers were patrolling their beats. When police officers failed to investigate serious crimes such as murders in their areas, Maple would push them for more evidence that they were working as hard as possible to make the right arrests. According to the NYPD, CompStat played a big role in reducing crime in the city from the 1990s onward. The system spread nationwide.

Maple wanted to make sure that race-class subjugated neighborhoods got the same protection from criminals that wealthier neighborhoods did. But his policy had an unintended effect. Police leaders figured out that by underreporting serious crime, and by arresting lots of people for small offenses, they could create data that made it seem like their policing work was especially effective.

The result was a workforce of police officers who felt they had to make a certain number of stops or arrests every day to justify their jobs. The officers were afraid to meet these quotas, or required numbers, by patrolling higher-income or mostly white neighborhoods. Wealthy people are more likely to have access to lawyers who can help them fight charges and fees, and white people may feel more empowered to argue in a court system that

Jack Maple, *right*, was a well-known officer in the NYPD.

MORE TO THE STORY

DOCUMENTING SEXUAL ASSAULT

According to the Rape, Abuse, and Incest National Network (RAINN), about one in every six women and one in every 33 men experience rape or attempted rape in the United States during their lifetimes.[13] People who have been sexually assaulted can choose to undergo a sexual assault forensic exam. These exams, also known as rape kits, collect evidence, such as signs of injury or DNA left on clothing, to assist with a potential criminal case. Police can then test the evidence from the kit to help find suspects.

In the United States, hundreds of thousands of rape kits have been collected but never tested. This buildup of unused evidence is called the rape kit backlog. The National Institute of Justice said that some kits aren't analyzed because the issue of consent is called into question. That is, the suspect says the sexual act was consensual, and officers think the rape kit wouldn't help with the investigation. In addition, sometimes the kits aren't analyzed if charges are dropped against suspects or if perpetrators plead guilty.

It is also common for victims of sexual assault to report that they faced discouragement or disbelief when reporting sexual assault to the police. A study by sociologist Martin Schwartz found that the average police officer did not believe about one-third of the reports of rape the officer encountered.[14] And a study of police departments in four major US cities found that the departments routinely undercounted reports of rape in their official documents.

treats them better than it does people of color. Stopping poor and minority citizens, and punishing them for infractions that other people might get away with, was seen by some as lower risk.

Several police departments across the United States adopted CompStat. The philosophy of using statistics to measure crime rates in certain areas and focusing relentlessly on bringing those rates down was influential. In addition, the kind of policing done in race-class subjugated neighborhoods created a large gap in the way different groups of Americans perceived the police. People in small communities may deeply value their police departments and see the police force as an integral part of the community. But people of color, and people in race-class subjugated communities in particular, are much more likely to have repeated negative interactions with police and to feel that the protection officers provide isn't meant for them.

"JACK WAS ONE OF THE TRULY GREAT INNOVATORS IN LAW ENFORCEMENT WHO HELPED TO MAKE NEW YORK CITY THE SAFEST LARGE CITY IN AMERICA."[15]

— RUDY GIULIANI, MAYOR OF NEW YORK CITY

CHAPTER SIX

POLICE BRUTALITY AND POLICIES

O n the evening of March 3, 1991, Rodney King was driving down the freeway in Los Angeles and got pulled over for speeding. He had alcohol in his system and was on parole at the time. He fled in his car, and police pursued him at high speeds. Eventually, he pulled over in front of an apartment building.

The police caught up with King there. A group of four police officers beat King for more than 15 minutes while a crowd of other officers watched. They broke King's bones, including his skull, and permanently damaged his brain. A man in the apartment building

Camera phones and social media have allowed more people to capture and share instances of police violence.

filmed the entire beating on his video camera and released it to the public.

The footage sparked an outcry, which intensified when the four officers charged with assaulting King were acquitted of almost all charges by a jury the next year. In April 1992, after the jury verdict, Los Angeles started to burn. People in the majority-Black area of South-Central Los Angeles began setting fires to buildings and attacking nonblack passersby. At first, the Los Angeles Police Department (LAPD) didn't respond at all to the riots. By the end of the violence five days later, more than 50 people had died and 2,000 were injured.[1]

"RACISM IS NOT GETTING WORSE. IT'S GETTING FILMED."[2]

—WILL SMITH, ACTOR AND PRODUCER

In the early 1900s, activists who protested police violence had no video recordings and few photographs to help publicize cases of abuse. In the 1960s, when the civil rights movement brought police brutality to the forefront of the national conversation, photos of police attacking protesters helped illustrate the struggle people of color faced in this regard. As technology advanced, so did the public's ability to raise awareness of police violence. The eyewitness evidence of King's beating would not have existed without the invention of portable video cameras.

COMMUNITY POLICING

As outrage grew over the unjust and violent treatment of Black people by some police officers, state and local governments began to rethink the hard-line War on Drugs approach. They brainstormed ways to foster connections between police and communities. Advocates of community policing began to find more of a foothold in the national conversation. According to the Bureau of Justice Assistance, which is a branch of the US Department of Justice, community policing is "a collaboration between the police and the community that identifies and solves

THE TALK

In some Black families, *the talk* is a phrase for conversations parents have with children about interacting with police. Many Black parents take on the responsibility of warning their children about the dangers of police violence. They give kids advice on how to minimize dangers when interacting with police. Psychiatrist Adrienne Clark recommends that parents start talking to their children about police brutality in an age-appropriate way when kids are in elementary school. She also recommends that Black parents remind their children that police may assume teenagers are older than they really are and that police might unfairly believe these children are more aggressive than their white counterparts.

community problems."[3] Community policing aims to give more control over conflict resolution to the community and get rid of tension and hostility between police and the people they serve.

During the early 1990s, Norm Stamper was working for the San Diego Police Department. After police in San Diego killed a man named Tommie DuBose in his home during a drug raid gone wrong, Stamper led a project to rethink the department's approach to policing. Things began to improve in the city. The department worked to build better ties with minority communities, sent officers out to work with the community, and opened more lines of communication for people to give honest feedback to police. Stamper saw these reforms as ways of bringing the department closer to the community policing ideal by integrating police officers into their patrol areas and reducing the power imbalances between police and citizens. Stamper's efforts

"THE EFFORT TO ACHIEVE AN AUTHENTIC PARTNERSHIP BETWEEN COMMUNITY AND POLICE . . . IS ALWAYS ON MY MIND. IT IS CRITICAL, IT SEEMS TO ME, THAT WE FIND A WAY TO FIND COMMON GROUND."[4]

—NORM STAMPER, FORMER SEATTLE, WASHINGTON, POLICE CHIEF AND SAN DIEGO COP

to spread his policing model to other cities were largely unsuccessful, as he found a lot of resistance from other police departments.

Like Stamper's reform efforts in San Diego, many community policing efforts were short-lived. In 1994, President Bill Clinton began a grant program called Community Oriented Policing Services, or COPS, to fund the hiring of community policing officers. The program gave departments nationwide about $1.5 billion a year through 1999, but it was not closely supervised.[5] Much of the money police departments received did not go to community policing.

The outcry caused by King's death faded, and while other incidents of police violence made the news, general support for the police remained high. According to the polling organization Gallup, from 1993 to 2017, the proportion of Americans who had a lot of confidence in police never dipped below 52 percent.[6] After the terrorist attacks of September 11, 2001, the US government shifted its focus from efforts on community policing to high-tech counterterrorism efforts. The USA Patriot Act, passed by Congress in 2001, gave more permission to

POLICE SURVEILLANCE OF MUSLIMS

After the September 11, 2001, terrorist attacks on New York City and Washington, DC, which had been carried out by Muslim extremists, the NYPD began a widespread surveillance campaign on local Muslim communities in New York, Pennsylvania, Connecticut, New Jersey, and other places. The department sent undercover officers to spy on Muslim organizations, opened and read the emails of Muslim college students, and pointed secret video cameras at mosques, among other measures. This surveillance was based on the prejudiced idea that Muslims in general should be treated as potential future terrorists. Muslims in the area sued the city, reporting that they felt unsafe and spied on in their homes and spiritual spaces. The NYPD said it would change its practices.

law enforcement agencies, including local police, to use tactics such as electronic surveillance and wiretapping to monitor suspects.

MICHAEL BROWN AND THE BLACK LIVES MATTER MOVEMENT

In August 2014, a man in Ferguson, Missouri, stole a pack of cigarillos from a convenience store and shoved the clerk who tried to stop him. Police officer Darren Wilson ran into 18-year-old Michael Brown, who was unarmed, and suspected him of committing the crime. A witness to the event later said that Brown ran toward Wilson, who then shot and killed Brown. His body was left in the street for hours before it was moved.

Brown's death spurred another wave of protests against police brutality. The year before, Alicia Garza, Opal Tometi, and Patrisse Cullors had started the Black Lives Matter movement to protest the acquittal of a man who killed an unarmed Black teenager named Trayvon

Thousands of people took to the streets to protest Michael Brown's death.

Martin. During the protests in Ferguson, activists used Black Lives Matter as a rallying cry.

US attorney general Eric Holder released a statement on the killing, expressing sympathy for Brown's family and the need to investigate any possible wrongdoing. "Aggressively pursuing investigations such as this is critical for preserving trust between law enforcement and the communities they serve," Holder said.[7]

The Black Lives Matter movement grew quickly online. Hashtags and viral videos got its message out. People from all walks of life had a medium that helped them share news, information, photos, and videos in real time. People didn't have to wait for a local news report to get quick information on police brutality protests. Now, it was right

THE WAR ON TERROR AND MILITARY EQUIPMENT

In the 2000s, local police departments received grants to buy the same military equipment and weapons at home that were being used in overseas wars. In many cases, this equipment ended up in areas where there was little use for it. For example, in 2012, the town of Keene, New Hampshire, bought a large armored vehicle with money from the federal government. In order to receive the money, the town had to explain why it needed help dealing with potential terrorist threats. The vehicle purchase was controversial in Keene, as critics argued that it was unnecessary in a small area with few terrorist targets. Keene is a town of approximately 23,000 people, according to 2018 US Census estimates.[8]

Michael Brown's memorial was reconstructed on July 30, 2020.

there on the internet. As DeRay Mckesson, a prominent

Black Lives Matter activist, explained, "The tools that we

have to organize and to resist are fundamentally different

than anything that's existed before in Black struggle."[9]

CHAPTER SEVEN

A NEW
MOVEMENT

Forty-six-year-old George Floyd went to a store in Minneapolis, Minnesota, to buy a pack of cigarettes on May 25, 2020. The clerk believed he paid with a counterfeit bill and called the police. When the police showed up minutes later, one officer drew his gun and Floyd was arrested and handcuffed. Floyd had complied with officers through most of the encounter. When the police tried to get him into the back of their car, Floyd stiffened and told them he was claustrophobic. A struggle occurred, and officers wrestled Floyd to the ground.

By that time, two more officers had arrived on the scene. One of them, Derek Chauvin, knelt on Floyd's

Signs are laid down in front of a mural of George Floyd after a demonstration in Manchester, United Kingdom. Floyd's killing created worldwide discussions about the roles of police.

neck for around eight minutes. Floyd said he couldn't breathe and asked to be released. Chauvin and the other officers didn't release Floyd. The Hennepin County medical examiner's autopsy found that Floyd died due to cardiopulmonary arrest complicated by police restraint. A local bystander filmed Floyd's death on her phone. Her video went viral online. Suddenly the nation and the world were seeing another Black person's death at the hands of police.

"I CAN'T BREATHE."[1]

—GEORGE FLOYD TO POLICE OFFICERS KNEELING ON HIM

Protests sprang up across the United States. At first, the demonstrations were about Floyd's death. They soon widened to address police brutality in general and then began to represent a nationwide reckoning surrounding systemic racism.

At this time, the world was also in the grips of the COVID-19 pandemic. In the United States, the pandemic was wreaking havoc on low-income communities, as a disproportionate number of Black and Hispanic people were dying from the virus at alarmingly high rates. These disparities were partly due to the effects of systemic racism. For example, Black and Hispanic people are more likely to work in customer service jobs, therefore making it more likely for them to come into contact with the virus, and they are less likely to have access to high-quality health care.

The protests spread across the United States and the world. One estimate found that by the beginning of July 2020, as many as 26 million Americans had participated in some form of protest inspired by Floyd.[2] In major cities, large-scale protests extended for weeks, riots occurred, and clashes with police left many people injured or arrested. A *Los Angeles Times* investigation found that LA protesters suffered "a range of injuries at the hands of the LAPD, from minor bruising from baton strikes and falls as police skirmish lines advanced, to

POLICING AND KETAMINE

The 2020 protests put the national spotlight on the death of 23-year-old Elijah McClain, a young man in Colorado who was killed by police in 2019. McClain, who was Black, was walking back from a convenience store when a bystander reported him as suspicious. Police officers found him and, when he became scared and agitated, said McClain was resisting arrest. A medical first responder injected him with 500 mg of ketamine, a powerful sedative with a recommended maximum dose of 250 mg. He died days later. The Adams County coroner said the cause of McClain's death was undetermined.

Ketamine is a controlled substance, and it is used illegally to produce feelings of euphoria and hallucinations. Police officers in Minnesota as well as Colorado have instructed EMTs to inject patients with ketamine against their will. According to lawyer Mari Newman, "I think ketamine has been weaponized particularly against people of color."[3]

serious injuries to their genitals and heads from foam and sponge bullets and beanbags being launched into crowds, sometimes from close range."[4]

Police officers across the country were getting harmed in violent protests too. In Washington, DC, more than 150 federal and local police sustained injuries while working at protests during the week after Floyd's death.[5] Around 350 NYPD officers were injured in the first two weeks of protests.[6] One officer was hit by a car. Others had bricks or fire extinguishers thrown at their heads by protesters. During one riot in July 2020 in Chicago, 18 officers were hurt after protesters threw bottles, rocks, and fireworks at them.[7]

TEAR GAS AND RUBBER BULLETS

Beginning with the civil unrest of the 1960s and 1970s, police used certain tactics to disperse people at protests. Two common police riot weapons, tear gas and rubber bullets, were both present at many of the 2020 protests. Tear gas irritates the eyes and makes it temporarily difficult for people to see. Rubber bullets hit the skin and cause painful welts. Although both tear gas and rubber bullets are often described as nonlethal weapons, they can severely injure and even kill people.

CALLS TO ABOLISH THE POLICE

During the same period of mourning and outrage over Floyd's death, another case of police violence came to light. Breonna Taylor, a 26-year-old emergency medical technician (EMT), was killed by police officers at her home in Louisville, Kentucky, months before the Floyd incident. Police had a no-knock warrant to search her apartment. When they entered, Taylor's boyfriend, Kenneth Walker, fired at police. The police fired back, resulting in Taylor's death. Walker later told police he fired his gun because he believed an intruder was entering the apartment.

On September 23, 2020, a grand jury charged one officer with endangering Taylor's neighbors during the night of the raid. The other officers were not charged. Kentucky attorney general Daniel Cameron said the

The deaths of George Floyd and Breonna Taylor at the hands of police attracted national attention and led to serious conversations about police reform.

officers had justification for shooting into Taylor's apartment since Walker shot at them first. Protests erupted in Louisville over the decisions. While some protests were peaceful, others were not. The night after the jury's decisions, two police officers were shot.

Noname is a rapper and activist with a strong social media presence. She has more than half a million followers on Twitter and often writes about social justice, racism, and politics. Noname stated that although she wanted to see justice for Taylor, she didn't support arresting the police officers who killed her. "I don't want the cop in jail. We've jailed cops before," Noname wrote. "I want the system that put the badge on his chest and the gun in his hand abolished."[8] In other words, Noname is a police abolitionist, someone who believes that policing in its current form should no longer exist.

To abolish something is to put a stop to it completely. Mariame Kaba is an organizer, writer, and a leading advocate of abolishing police and prisons, or what she calls the criminal punishment system. Kaba grew up in a low-income neighborhood in New York City but attended a private French high school uptown, where she was a Black student in a majority-white and -affluent environment. Kaba noticed that while her friends from school tended to use drugs more often than her neighborhood friends and relatives, they were never arrested by police, while people in her neighborhood were.

Kaba views policing and prisons as harmful institutions, believes that policing should be eliminated, and believes that the money spent on police departments should go to social services, such as providing addiction centers and shelters for homeless people. She also thinks that the role of patrolling, the core of a police officer's daily work, is better suited to people who live inside the community and have ties to its

THE OVERTON WINDOW

The Overton window is a public policy concept invented by scholar Joseph Overton. It proposes that there are two types of ideas: ones that are within the range of acceptable public opinion, a range known as the Overton window, and ones that are not. For instance, in the area of police reform, a call to reduce police budgets is inside the Overton window. This means that not everyone supports the idea, but it is seen as socially acceptable. A proposal to bring back the old voluntary night-watch system, however, is outside the Overton window, since night watches are seen as very outdated. Overton believed that politicians could only enact policies that fit inside the Overton window. People with ideas outside the window had to wait until shifts in public opinion made their views possible to discuss seriously.

residents. In other words, Kaba believes that community members should be more involved with and accountable for each other, with regular people taking on the daily work of law enforcement and public safety.

Paul H. Robinson, a law professor at the University of Pennsylvania, is not in favor of abolishing the police. He notes that there are people who will take advantage of a no-punishment system to further their own interests. "Dismantling mechanisms of coercive enforcement is not a wacky idea, but neither is it a successful one. Whether we like it or not, human nature is such that coercive enforcement of rules is indispensable to protect the rights of all."[10]

While many people do not believe in getting rid of police, public opinion has shifted drastically in favor of

POLICE PROTESTS AND POPULAR MUSIC

There's a long history of protests against police violence in US music, especially in hip-hop. Perhaps the most famous anti-police song is "F—— tha Police," released by rap group N.W.A in 1988. The song expressed the rappers' rage at the way they'd been treated by police while growing up in Compton, California, a largely race-class subjugated community. The song has had renewed popularity as a protest anthem. Also, in 2020, rapper DaBaby reached Number 1 with his hit song "Rockstar." He decided to release a Black Lives Matter remix of the song, where he raps about abuse of police power.

Protests in Portland, Oregon, lasted for more than 100 days after Floyd's death. Some protesters called for the abolishment of the police department.

police reform in a short amount of time. A June 2020 poll by the Associated Press-NORC Center for Public Affairs Research found that almost all Americans supported some type of police reform. The poll also found more people thought police brutality was a major problem in the country compared with those polled in 2015. Almost 70 percent of respondents said they thought the police system needed either major changes or a complete overhaul.[11] In June 2020, the Minneapolis City Council pledged to dismantle its police department. People were faced with the question of what steps should come next.

FROM THE
HEADLINES

THE DEATH OF BREONNA TAYLOR

Just after midnight on March 13, 2020, Breonna Taylor was asleep in her apartment in Louisville, Kentucky, her boyfriend, Kenneth Walker, at her side. Taylor was a 26-year-old EMT.

Taylor and her boyfriend woke up when a team of police officers entered her apartment, breaking in the door with a battering ram. Walker, a licensed gun owner, fired his gun at them. Police fired back, and at least eight bullets struck Taylor. She died that night. The officers had legal permission to enter Taylor's apartment that night using what's known as a no-knock warrant.

Typically, police need a warrant, or written permission from a court, in order to search someone's home. To respect a suspects' right to safety and privacy in their own houses, police are usually required to announce themselves and get permission to come inside and conduct their search. However, in the 1960s, legislators began to

Many people wanted justice for Breonna Taylor. They demanded the arrest of the officers and called for an end to no-knock warrants.

authorize no-knock raids, which allowed police to enter homes with little or no notice. A 1963 Supreme Court decision ruled that these raids were legal when police had reason to believe the raid could minimize time for suspects to get rid of evidence, such as drugs hidden inside their homes. A court authorized the no-knock raid that killed Taylor because police believed her ex-boyfriend, Jamarcus Glover, was receiving drug shipments at the apartment. Glover was arrested separately the same night, and Taylor was not believed to be a danger to others or even involved in the case. Taylor's family filed a wrongful death lawsuit against the city. Louisville officials agreed to pay $12 million to her family and to enact some changes to the police department.[12]

CHAPTER EIGHT

POLICE
REFORMS

An August 2020 poll conducted by the Minneapolis *Star Tribune* followed up with the city's residents to get their thoughts on how Minneapolis should move ahead with reforming the police. The poll found that most Minneapolis residents supported reassigning some police tasks to other organizations. About 75 percent of the people polled said they wanted to see some police funding go to social service organizations that help people with problems such as drug addiction and homelessness.[1] In other words, there was a great deal of support for the idea of defunding Minneapolis police. Defunding means reducing financial support. Some people believe in shrinking police budgets as an intermediate

Activists attend a city council meeting in Norman, Oklahoma, to encourage the council to defund the police.

step toward getting rid of police altogether, while others support the idea of a smaller and therefore less politically powerful police force but oppose abolition.

However, the poll also found that some people did not support shrinking the city's police force. Only 35 percent of Black respondents thought the Minneapolis police department should have fewer people. Some residents were concerned that without the police, they might lack protection from crime. "[If there are fewer police,] it's going to take them longer to get there and by then the perpetrator is gone," explained Sam Brown, a Black man who lives in Minneapolis.[2]

Minneapolis and other cities across the county face a series of questions moving forward. Some people wonder whether police departments should exist at all. If they do exist, people question how much power they should have and how departments should be funded. There are also

8CANTWAIT

In the wake of the George Floyd protests, an organization called Campaign Zero released a policy plan called 8CantWait. Campaign Zero was founded after the Black Lives Matter protests in Ferguson, and it advocates for the end of police violence. 8CantWait was a plan aimed at reducing the likelihood of police brutality by enacting eight policy and rule changes. Most of the changes revolved around requiring police to use force less often.

conversations about which policing jobs are necessary and whether there are police functions that other people or organizations should be doing instead. Many people wonder what a different public safety and law enforcement system would look like.

THE DEBATE OVER BODY CAMERAS

One widespread but controversial innovation in the world of police reform is the body camera. Body cameras are worn by police on duty to record their actions. After Michael Brown's death, his family members spoke out about their belief that police needed body cameras as objective records for their interactions with citizens. People who are interested in police accountability, or holding

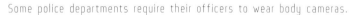
Some police departments require their officers to wear body cameras.

police more responsible for misconduct, see body cameras as a useful solution.

Body cameras require police officers to film themselves on the job. The Rialto, California, police department was the first to require body cameras. In 2012, it began asking about half of its officers to wear them on the job. The department saw remarkable results. There was a decline of almost 90 percent in complaints against officers after a year. A 2019 survey of body camera research by George Mason University found that some studies showed a decrease in police use of force due to body cameras, though others showed no real difference. The survey also found that police often liked using body cameras to have evidence for their perspectives on different encounters. "I think it protects me more than it protects the public," Rialto cop Gary Cunningham said.[3]

Critics of body cameras, however, point out that video evidence is not immune to bias or misrepresentation. Regulations about the use of body cameras varies widely across departments. Additionally, body camera skeptics point out that cameras cannot help address some of the systemic inequalities of policing, such as incentives for police to patrol more heavily in low-income areas. They cannot stop suspicion and hostility between community members and police before tense situations begin.

DEFUNDING POLICE AND REASSIGNING RESPONSIBILITIES

Supporters of defunding the police tend to agree that some of the money that currently goes to police budgets should be spent on social and public services, such as education. Advocates say doing this would help stop crime at its source. For example, people with untreated mental disorders, such as schizophrenia, have a greater tendency to behave erratically and are at an increased risk of serving jail time for infractions such as disrupting the peace.

POLICING AND EMT WORK

The work of EMTs is an example of a former police job that became a separate social service over time. Police officers used to be responsible for answering emergency medical calls. In some racially segregated areas, police weren't responding to emergency calls, causing residents to miss out on crucial medical care. In Pittsburgh, Pennsylvania, in the 1960s, a group of residents created the Freedom House Ambulance Service to help with medical emergencies in the majority-Black Hill District. Eventually, Pittsburgh took on the service as its own, and the EMT unit was born.

FROM THE
HEADLINES

JACOB BLAKE AND RENEWED CALLS FOR CHANGE

Kenosha, Wisconsin, is a majority-white city, with a Black population of about 11.5 percent.[4] On August 23, 2020, police in the city responded to a 911 call about a domestic disturbance. The Wisconsin Department of Justice Division of Criminal Investigation says a woman phoned police to say "her boyfriend was present and was not supposed to be on the premises."[5] When police arrived on the scene, they tried to arrest a 29-year-old Black man named Jacob Blake. The department says Blake went to his car and leaned forward. In a bystander video, one officer can be heard telling Blake to drop a knife. However, the video did not show whether Blake was holding a knife, though one was later found on his car floor. One of the responding officers shot Blake in the back several times.

Blake was sent to the hospital and survived the shooting. But he was paralyzed and cannot walk, he suffered organ

The Washington Mystics wore shirts spelling out Jacob Blake's name. The shirts also had markings that represented bullet holes on the backs.

damage, and he had to have much of his small intestine removed. Two officers involved in the 911 response were placed on administrative leave. This means that they were not fired and would still be paid, but they were not expected to work for the duration of the leave.

The Kenosha police department does not require body cameras, but a bystander filmed the shooting. As with previous cases of police brutality, news of the shooting spread quickly on social media. Blake's shooting ignited a wave of protests within Kenosha, as well as counterprotests in support of police. Someone shot three protesters, killing two of them. A 17-year-old, Kyle Rittenhouse, was charged in August of killing the two people. Many professional athletes spoke out against Blake's shooting and the ongoing problems of racial inequality and police brutality. The National Basketball Association and Women's National Basketball Association postponed their games in protest of Blake's shooting.

Although most people with mental disorders are not violent, they may make other people uncomfortable with their behaviors, and they may have trouble interacting with police and following commands. Xochitl Villarrealis described how his brother with schizophrenia, who was experiencing homelessness, ended up having multiple negative encounters with police, although his brother was not a threat: "It was very common for people to call the police when they saw my brother," Villarrealis explains. "Along with his appearance and inability to comprehend the situation sometimes, some police officers moved very quickly to arrest him."[6]

These encounters can be extremely dangerous. According to the Treatment Advocacy Center, a nonprofit organization that strives to help individuals who have mental illnesses, people with severe mental illnesses are approximately 16 times likelier than those who don't to face police violence.[7] But there are publicly funded alternatives for helping people who are suffering from mental health crises. In Eugene, Oregon, for example, the organization Crisis Assistance Helping Out On the Streets (CAHOOTS) responds to such cases by sending an unarmed pair of health-care workers to offer assistance. In addition, reducing the pressure on police to make frequent arrests and stops could help protect vulnerable people from repeated stops for small infractions, which in turn would decrease the likelihood of violent encounters.

NEW IDEAS FOR LAW ENFORCEMENT

Alex Tabarrok is a professor at George Mason University. He believes the law enforcement system should change so that there are fewer armed interactions between police and citizens in general. Tabarrok gives the example of traffic laws. Police are armed with guns when they patrol roads and highways. In fact, traffic

WHAT SOCIAL WORKERS DO

Many government social services are provided by social workers. Social work as a profession began around the beginning of the 1900s. It was designed to help solve problems for people from poor and immigrant communities. One of the most famous early social workers, Jane Addams, built a series of houses where middle- and upper-class people lived alongside poorer people and helped provide social services such as health care and childcare.

Today, some social workers can find jobs as therapists, work for the government, or work for nonprofits that focus on substance abuse treatment or child protective services. While some people believe that social workers could take on some of the patrolling functions of police, others think that they are not equipped for the job. One social worker, who goes by the name R., believes that social workers carry many of the same biases police do. Also, social workers are already prone to burnout, or stress from chronic overwork, without added tasks to their workloads.

stops are the leading causes of interactions between police and citizens. And since these interactions occur while police are armed, they have the potential to escalate quickly. The death of Philando Castile, a Black man shot by police in 2016, was one of many that resulted during a routine traffic stop.

Tabarrok isn't the only one looking at ways to improve policing. In the past few decades, people in communities plagued by violent crime have begun to come up with new ways of creating accountability and reform. The organization Cure Violence began in Chicago, a city with high rates of murder and gun violence. It took root in 2000, in a violent Chicago neighborhood called West Garfield Park, where it was able to reduce shooting deaths by 67 percent in one year.[8]

Cure Violence hires unarmed staff called violence interrupters and outreach workers. Its approach has three main branches. First, when violence does occur, Cure Violence tries to break a cycle of escalation and retaliation by meeting with everyone involved and managing conflict. Second, outreach workers try to identify people at special risk of violence and get them the help they need. And third, the organization works to change local culture so that violence is taken very seriously and is seen as unacceptable. Cure Violence works in various cities across the United States and the world. It has a track record of reducing shooting deaths in a short amount of time. However, the organization focuses on specific neighborhoods, and it works as a prevention tool, not an emergency service. People cannot call upon organizations such as Cure Violence in the face of immediate threats.

"HAVING WITNESSED A RACIST POLICE SYSTEM FROM THE INSIDE, I UNDERSTAND WHY PEOPLE ARE DESPERATE FOR CHANGE. SOME ARE CALLING FOR THE DISSOLUTION OF POLICING ALTOGETHER. AS A BLACK PERSON, I UNDERSTAND. AS A COP, I THINK THAT'S THE WRONG ANSWER."[9]

—DAVID HUGHES, POLICE OFFICER IN NEWPORT NEWS, VIRGINIA

Debates about policing center around safety, justice, harm, and responsibility. They bring up central questions about how US society runs. As policing evolves, there are many opportunities for all Americans to join the conversation about how to address past injustices and talk about what kind of policing system they'd like to see in the future.

ESSENTIAL FACTS

MAJOR EVENTS

- Policing in the United States evolves from both European traditions and from slave patrols. The first professional police force in the country is established in 1838.

- In the 1950s and 1960s, the civil rights movement brings attention to police brutality in the United States.

- In 1971, President Richard Nixon launches the War on Drugs campaign. This allows police officers to aggressively target drug users and sellers.

- In the 1990s, people try to improve policing by building better ties with communities.

- In 1994, Rudy Giuliani becomes New York City's mayor. He implements a controversial stop-and-frisk policy to help lower crime.

- A 2019 report by the *Proceedings of the National Academy of Sciences* finds that various minority groups in the United States are more likely to be killed by police than white people are.

KEY PLAYERS

- Police officers have a lot of responsibilities. They respond to emergencies and reports of crime. They also try to prevent crimes from happening.

- Police unions protect the interests of police officers.

- New York City police officer Jack Maple develops CompStat in the 1990s to fight crime in his city.

- In 2018, a school resource officer in Noblesville, Indiana, responds to a school shooting and helps a teacher who has been shot.

IMPACT ON SOCIETY

Police officers have many roles and responsibilities. Some serve as school resource officers to keep students and staff safe. Officers in the community keep public order, respond to crimes, enforce laws, patrol the roads, and do much more. They handle threats to keep communities safe, which can sometimes land them in difficult situations. Police have been heavily criticized for perceived acts of brutality. People debate over whether policing in the United States should change.

QUOTE

"At the end of the day, our goal is to help people. . . . My goal isn't just to become a police officer just to arrest people and lock up the bad guys."

—*Darry Jones, police officer in Columbia Heights, Minnesota*

GLOSSARY

ACQUIT
To clear a person of the charges that have been brought against him or her.

BIAS
Prejudice in favor of or against one thing, person, or group compared with another, usually in a way considered to be unfair.

CIVIL RIGHTS
Enforceable privileges of citizens to personal and political liberties such as freedom of speech, the right to vote, and social equality.

DEFUND
To withdraw funding.

DISPROPORTIONATE
Out of proportion in size, number, or effect; too large or too small in comparison with what would be expected or justified.

ESCALATE

To increase in intensity.

FELONY

A crime more serious than a misdemeanor, usually punishable by imprisonment.

PATROL

To move around an assigned area, looking for disturbances or problems.

PROBATION

A period of time at a job when a person's superiors observe him or her to see whether the person does well in a certain role.

RACE-CLASS SUBJUGATION

Oppression on the basis of both race and class, such as when people have low incomes and are treated unfairly based on their race.

WARRANT

A document allowing law enforcement to carry out an arrest, a search, or an information-gathering operation.

ADDITIONAL
RESOURCES

SELECTED BIBLIOGRAPHY

Balko, Radley. *Rise of the Warrior Cop: The Militarization of America's Police Forces.* PublicAffairs, 2013.

Palmiotto, Michael J., et al. *McGraw-Hill Education Police Officer Exams.* McGraw Hill Education, 2018.

Soss, Joe, and Vesla Weaver. "Police Are Our Government: Politics, Political Science, and the Policing of Race-Class Subjugated Communities." *Annual Review of Political Science,* May 2017, annualreviews.org. Accessed 21 Oct. 2020.

FURTHER READINGS

Brandl, Steven G. *Police in America.* SAGE, 2021.

Harris, Duchess, with Alexis Burling. *The Killing of George Floyd.* Abdo, 2021.

Harris, Duchess, with Rebecca Rissman. *Race and Policing.* Abdo, 2018.

ONLINE RESOURCES

To learn more about policing in America, please visit **abdobooklinks.com** or scan this QR code. These links are routinely monitored and updated to provide the most current information available.

MORE INFORMATION

For more information on this subject, contact or visit the following organizations:

American Civil Liberties Union
125 Broad St., Eighteenth Floor
New York, NY 10004
212-549-2500
aclu.org
The American Civil Liberties Union (ACLU) advocates for civil rights in the United States. It offers information and guidance to people affected by police brutality or discrimination, or who are curious about their rights.

International Association of Chiefs of Police
44 Canal Center Plaza #200
Alexandria, VA 22314
703-836-6767
theiacp.org
The International Association of Chiefs of Police offers resources and information for current police officers as well as people interested in police careers.

SOURCE
NOTES

CHAPTER 1. SAFE AT SCHOOL?

1. Arika Herron. "It's Been a Year Since the Noblesville School Shooting. Here's How Indiana Has Changed." *Indy Star*, 21 May 2019, indystar.com. Accessed 13 Oct. 2020.

2. Holly V. Hays. "Indianapolis Police Officer on Leave after Video Shows Him Appearing to Strike Shortridge Student." *Indy Star*, 30 Aug. 2019, indystar.com. Accessed 13 Oct. 2020.

3. Dana Goldstein. "Do Police Officers Make Schools Safer or More Dangerous?" *New York Times*, 12 June 2020, nytimes.com. Accessed 13 Oct. 2020.

4. Dylan Peers McCoy and Stephanie Wang. "School Police More Than Twice As Likely to Arrest Black Students in Indiana." *IBJ*, 24 June 2020, ibj.com. Accessed 13 Oct. 2020.

5. "Spare the Rod." *APM Reports*, 25 Aug. 2016, apmreports.org. Accessed 15 Oct. 2020.

6. "10 Years. 180 School Shootings." *CNN*, n.d., cnn.com. Accessed 21 Oct. 2020.

7. West Resendes. "Police in Schools Continue to Target Black, Brown, and Indigenous Students with Disabilities." *ACLU*, 9 July 2020, aclu.org. Accessed 21 Oct. 2020.

8. Resendes, "Police in Schools Continue to Target Black, Brown, and Indigenous Students with Disabilities."

9. Claire Bryan. "Police Don't Make Most Black Students Feel Safer, Survey Shows." *Chalkbeat*, 8 June 2020, chalkbeat.org. Accessed 13 Oct. 2020.

10. Nicole Chavez. "5 Students Tell You Why They Want Police-Free Schools." *CNN*, 28 June 2020, cnn.com. Accessed 13 Oct. 2020.

11. Amelia Thomson-DeVeaux and Maggie Koerth. "Is Police Reform a Fundamentally Flawed Idea?" *FiveThirtyEight*, 22 June 2020, fivethirtyeight.com. Accessed 13 Oct. 2020.

12. Frank Edwards et al. "Risk of Being Killed by Police Use of Force in the US by Age, Race/Ethnicity, and Sex." *Prison Policy*, 2 Aug. 2019, prisonpolicy.com. Accessed 13 Oct. 2020.

13. "Juvenile Arrests." *Office of Justice Programs*, n.d., ojjdp.gov. Accessed 13 Oct. 2020.

14. Rodd Wagner. "Spare a Thought for the Good Cops." *Forbes*, 31 May 2020, forbes.com. Accessed 13 Oct. 2020.

CHAPTER 2. THE HISTORY OF POLICING

1. Leonard Moore. "Police Brutality in the United States." *Britannica*, 27 July 2020, britannica.com. Accessed 13 Oct. 2020.

2. "History of Lynchings." *NAACP*, n.d., naacp.org. Accessed 13 Oct. 2020.

3. "Reconstruction in America." *Equal Justice Initiative*, 2015, eji.org. Accessed 13 Oct. 2020.

4. Katie Nodjimbadem. "The Long, Painful History of Police Brutality in the US." *Smithsonian*, 19 May 2020, smithsonianmag.com. Accessed 13 Oct. 2020.

5. David T. Hardy. "When Local Cops Drive Tanks: The Deadly Consequences of Militarizing Mayberry." *Salon*, 21 Oct. 2017, salon.com. Accessed 13 Oct. 2020.

6. "Hallandale Beach, Florida Population 2020." *World Population Review*, n.d., worldpopulationreview.com. Accessed 13 Oct. 2020.

7. "What Are Your Miranda Rights?" *Miranda Warning*, n.d., mirandawarning.org. Accessed 13 Oct. 2020.

8. Christian Parenti. *Lockdown America*. Verso, 2008. 70.

9. Christopher J. Coyne and Abigail R. Hall. "Four Decades and Counting: The Continued Failure of the War on Drugs." *Cato Institute*, 12 Apr. 2017, cato.org. Accessed 13 Oct. 2020.

CHAPTER 3. WHAT DO THE POLICE DO?

1. "Occupational Employment Statistics." *US Bureau of Labor Statistics*, n.d., bls.gov. Accessed 13 Oct. 2020.

2. Shelley S. Hyland and Elizabeth Davis. "Local Police Departments, 2016: Personnel." *Bureau of Justice Statistics*, 25 Oct. 2019, bjs.gov. Accessed 13 Oct. 2020.

3. Joshua Sargent. "'Defunding the Police' Isn't Simply about Taking Money Away, and This Book Explains It." *SFGATE*, 4 June 2020, sfgate.com. Accessed 13 Oct. 2020.

4. Hyland and Davis, "Local Police Departments, 2016."

5. Andrew DePietro. "Here's How Much Money Police Officers Earn in Every State." *Forbes*, 23 Apr. 2020, forbes.com. Accessed 13 Oct. 2020.

6. Officer Jones. "Here's Why I Became a Police Officer." *YouTube*, 14 Oct. 2018, youtube.com. Accessed 13 Oct. 2020.

7. Jess Scherman. "6 Often Overlooked Qualities of a Great Police Officer." *Rasmussen College*, 16 Sept. 2016, rasmussen.edu. Accessed 13 Oct. 2020.

8. Adam Conover. "The Cult of Policing and What Defunding Means with Larry Smith." *Earwolf*, 30 June 2020, earwolf.com. Accessed 13 Oct. 2020.

9. "Injuries, Illnesses, and Fatalities: Fact Sheet, Police Officers." *US Bureau of Labor Statistics*, 7 July 2020, bls.gov. Accessed 13 Oct. 2020.

10. Alicia Lee. "What It's Like to Be a Black Police Officer, Navigating Two Turbulent Worlds." *CNN*, 12 June 2020, cnn.com. Accessed 13 Oct. 2020.

CHAPTER 4. POLICE FUNDING, POWER, AND INFLUENCE

1. Daarel Burnette II. "Schools or Police: In Some Cities, a Reckoning on Spending Priorities." *Education Week*, 18 June 2020, edweek.org. Accessed 13 Oct. 2020.

2. Mandi Cai and Juan Pable Garnham. "Texas' Largest Cities Spend More on Police Than Anything Else." *Texas Tribune*, 14 Aug. 2020, texastribune.org. Accessed 13 Oct. 2020.

3. Keya Vakil. "Police Unions Are Preventing Real Reform. Here's How." *Courier*, 16 June 2020, couriernewsroom.com. Accessed 13 Oct. 2020.

4. Lauren Jackson. "An Interview with the Mayor of Minneapolis." *New York Times*, 19 Aug. 2020, nytimes.com. Accessed 15 Oct. 2020.

5. Emma Nolan. "'Cops' Cancelled: TV Show Has Been Accused of Racism Ever Since It First Aired 31 Years Ago." *Newsweek*, 10 June 2020, newsweek.com. Accessed 13 Oct. 2020.

6. Nancy Wang Yuen. "How Racial Stereotypes in Popular Media Affect People." *Scholars Strategy Network*, 4 June 2019, scholars.org. Accessed 13 Oct. 2020.

CHAPTER 5. RACE, CLASS, AND POLICING

1. "Rates of Drug Use and Sales, by Race." *Hamilton Project*, 21 Oct. 2016, hamiltonproject.org. Accessed 13 Oct. 2020.

2. "Stop-and-Frisk Data." *NYCLU*, n.d., nyclu.org. Accessed 13 Oct. 2020.

3. "Quick Facts: New York City, New York." *United States Census*, n.d., census.gov. Accessed 13 Oct. 2020.

4. "Stop-and-Frisk Data."

5. Deidre McPhillips. "Deaths from Police Harm Disproportionately Affect People of Color." *US News*, 3 June 2020, usnews.com. Accessed 13 Oct. 2020.

SOURCE NOTES CONTINUED

6. Reina Sultan. "6 People Describe Being Stopped and Frisked When Bloomberg Was Mayor of NYC." *Vice*, 21 Feb. 2020, vice.com. Accessed 13 Oct. 2020.

7. Martin Kaste. "New Study Says White Police Officers Are Not More Likely to Shoot Minority Suspects." *NPR*, 26 July 2019, npr.org. Accessed 13 Oct. 2020.

8. Frank Edwards et al. "Risk of Being Killed by Police Use of Force in the United States by Age, Race/Ethnicity, and Sex." *PNAS*, 20 Aug. 2019, pnas.org. Accessed 13 Oct. 2020.

9. Eliott C. McLaughlin. "Police Officers in the US Were Charged with More Than 400 Rapes Over a 9-Year Period." *CNN*, 19 Oct. 2018, cnn.com. Accessed 13 Oct. 2020.

10. Kaste, "New Study Says White Police Officers Are Not More Likely to Shoot Minority Suspects."

11. Larry Smith. "Police Are Trained to Fear." *Medium*, 26 Nov. 2018, gen.medium.com. Accessed 13 Oct. 2020.

12. "Racial Hoaxes: Black Men and Imaginary Crimes." *NPR*, 8 June 2009, npr.org. Accessed 13 Oct. 2020.

13. "Victims of Sexual Violence: Statistics." *RAINN*, n.d., rainn.org. Accessed 13 Oct. 2020.

14. Kate Harding. *Asking for It*. Da Capo Lifelong, 2015. 87.

15. Douglas Martin. "Jack Maple, 48, a Designer of City Crime Control Strategies." *New York Times*, 6 Aug. 2001, nytimes.com. Accessed 15 Oct. 2020.

CHAPTER 6. POLICE BRUTALITY AND POLICIES

1. Anjuli Sastry and Karen Grigsby Bates. "When LA Erupted in Anger: A Look Back at the Rodney King Riots." *NPR*, 26 Apr. 2017, npr.org. Accessed 13 Oct. 2020.

2. "Will Smith: 'Racism Is Not Getting Worse, It's Getting Filmed.'" *Hollywood Reporter*, 3 Aug. 2016, hollywoodreporter.com. Accessed 13 Oct. 2020.

3. "Understanding Community Policing." *Bureau of Justice Assistance*, Aug. 1994, ncjrs.gov. Accessed 13 Oct. 2020.

4. "Former Police Chief Has a Plan for 'How to Fix America's Police.'" *NPR*, 10 July 2016, npr.org. Accessed 21 Oct. 2020.

5. Radley Balko. "DOJ Agency Warns of Police Militarization." *HuffPost*, 9 Dec. 2013, huffpost.com. Accessed 13 Oct. 2020.

6. Jim Norman. "Confidence in Police Back at Historical Average." *Gallup*, 10 July 2017, news.gallup.com. Accessed 13 Oct. 2020.

7. David Hudson. "President Obama Issues a Statement on the Death of Michael Brown." *Obama White House*, 12 Aug. 2014, obamawhitehouse.archives.gov. Accessed 13 Oct. 2020.

8. "Keene, NH." *New Hampshire Employment Security*, n.d., nhes.nh.gov. Accessed 13 Oct. 2020.

9. Bijan Stephen. "Social Media Helps Black Lives Matter Fight the Power." *Wired*, n.d., wired.com. Accessed 13 Oct. 2020.

CHAPTER 7. A NEW MOVEMENT

1. Maanvi Singh. "George Floyd Told Officers 'I Can't Breathe' More Than 20 Times, Transcripts Show." *Guardian*, 9 July 2020, theguardian.com. Accessed 13 Oct. 2020.

2. Larry Buchanan et al. "Black Lives Matter May Be the Largest Movement in US History." *New York Times*, 3 July 2020, nytimes.com. Accessed 13 Oct. 2020.

3. Angelina Chapin. "Is Ketamine the New Police Weapon against Black Lives?" *Cut*, 30 June 2020, thecut.com. Accessed 13 Oct. 2020.

4. Kevin Rector et al. "LAPD's Use of Batons, Other Weapons Appears to Violate Rules, Significantly Injuring Protesters, Times Review Finds." *Los Angeles Times*, 11 June 2020, latimes.com. Accessed 13 Oct. 2020.

5. Eliana Block. "Yes, At Least 150 Local and Federal Officers Were Injured During the First Week of Protests in DC." *WUSA9*, 11 June 2020, wusa9.com. Accessed 13 Oct. 2020.

6. Tom Winter and Jonathan Dienst. "Nearly 400 NYPD Cops Hurt During NYC's Two Weeks of Protest over George Floyd's Death." *NBC New York*, 11 June 2020, nbcnewyork.com. Accessed 13 Oct. 2020.

7. Madeline Holcombe et al. "18 Police Officers Were Hurt in a Chicago Protest." *CNN*, 18 July 2020, cnn.com. Accessed 13 Oct. 2020.

8. Noname. "I don't want the cop in jail. We've jailed cops before. I want the system that put the badge on his chest and the gun in his hand abolished." *Twitter*, 23 July 2020, twitter.com. Accessed 13 Oct. 2020.

9. Asad Haider. "No Justice, No Peace." *Viewpoint Magazine*, 4 June 2020, viewpointmag.com. Accessed 13 Oct. 2020.

10. Paul H. Robinson. "Don't Abolish the Police." *USA Today*, 21 June 2020, usatoday.com. Accessed 13 Oct. 2020.

11. Andrea Cipriano. "95 Percent of Americans Want Police Reform: Poll." *Crime Report*, 23 June 2020, thecrimereport.org. Accessed 13 Oct. 2020.

12. Rukmini Callimachi. "Breonna Taylor's Family to Receive $12 Million Settlement from City of Louisville." *New York Times*, 2 Oct. 2020, nytimes.com. Accessed 13 Oct. 2020.

CHAPTER 8. POLICE REFORMS

1. Eric Roper. "Poll: Cuts to Minneapolis Police Ranks Lack Majority Support." *Star Tribune*, 15 Aug. 2020, startribune.com. Accessed 13 Oct. 2020.

2. Roper, "Poll: Cuts to Minneapolis Police Ranks Lack Majority Support."

3. Dina Demetrius and Michael Okwu. "Meet the First US Police Department to Deploy Body Cameras." *Aljazeera America*, 17 Dec. 2014, america.aljazeera.com. Accessed 13 Oct. 2020.

4. "Quick Facts: Kenosha City, Wisconsin." *United States Census*, n.d., census.gov. Accessed 13 Oct. 2020.

5. Karma Allen and Sabina Ghebremedhin. "Family, Investigators and Police Offer Starkly Different Views of Jacob Blake in Wake of Police Shooting." *ABC News*, 1 Sept. 2020, abcnews.go.com. Accessed 13 Oct. 2020.

6. Xochitl Villarrealis. "My Brother Is Not a Threat, He Has Schizophrenia." *NAMI*, 15 Mar. 2019, nami.org. Accessed 13 Oct. 2020.

7. "US Mentally Ill 16 Times More Likely to Be Killed by Police: Study." *Reuters*, 10 Dec. 2015, reuters.com. Accessed 13 Oct. 2020.

8. "Cure Violence to Establish New NGO." *CVG*, 18 Apr. 2019, cvg.org. Accessed 13 Oct. 2020.

9. David Hughes. "I'm a Black Police Officer. Here's How to Change the System." *New York Times*, 16 July 2020, nytimes.com. Accessed 13 Oct. 2020.

INDEX

ABOUT THE
AUTHORS

DUCHESS HARRIS, JD, PhD

Dr. Harris is a professor of American Studies and Political Science at Macalester College and curator of the Duchess Harris Collection of ABDO books. She is also the coauthor of the collection, which features popular titles such as *Hidden Human Computers: The Black Women of NASA* and series including Freedom's Promise and Race and American Law. In addition, Dr. Harris hosts the Freedom's Promise podcast with her son.

Before working with ABDO, Dr. Harris authored several other books on the topics of race, culture, and American history. She served as an associate editor for *Litigation News*, the American Bar Association Section of Litigation's quarterly flagship publication, and was the first editor in chief of *Law Raza*, an interactive online journal covering race and the law, published at William Mitchell College of Law. She has earned a BA in History from the University of Pennsylvania, a PhD in American Studies from the University of Minnesota, and a JD from William Mitchell College of Law.

A.W. BUCKEY

A.W. Buckey is a writer and pet sitter living in Brooklyn, New York.